Little Business Books

Creativity

Written by **Ruth Percival**
Illustrated by **Dean Gray**

Published in 2026 by Windmill Books,
an Imprint of Rosen Publishing
2544 Clinton St.
Buffalo, NY 14224

First published in Great Britain in 2024 by Hodder & Stoughton
Copyright © Hodder & Stoughton Limited, 2024

Credits
Series Editor: Amy Pimperton
Series Designer: Peter Scoulding
Consultant: Philippa Anderson

Philippa Anderson has a business degree and is a writer and communications consultant who advises multinationals. She authors and contributes to business books.

Cataloging-in-Publication Data

Names: Percival, Ruth, author. | Grey, Dean, illustrator.
Title: Creativity / Ruth Percival, illustrated by Dean Grey.
Description: Buffalo, NY : Windmill Books, 2026. | Series: Little business books | Includes glossary and index.
Identifiers: ISBN 9781725396463 (pbk.) | ISBN 9781725396470 (library bound) | ISBN 9781725396487 (ebook)
Subjects: LCSH: Creative ability--Juvenile literature. | Success in business--Juvenile literature.
Classification: LCC BF723.C7 P478 2026 | DDC 155.4'1335--dc23

All rights reserved.

All facts and statistics were up to date at the time of press.

No part of this book may be reproduced in any form without permission in writing from the publisher, except by a reviewer.

Printed in the United States of America

CPSIA Compliance Information: Batch #CSWM26
For Further Information contact Rosen Publishing at 1-800-237-9932

Contents

4	What Is Creativity?
6	Brainstorm Ideas
8	Have Fun Experimenting
10	Learn New Skills
12	Everyone Is Creative
14	Create Change
16	Stand Out
18	Be Inspired
20	Fail … and Try Again
22	Ask for Help
24	Try New Ideas
26	Take a Break
28	Celebrate Together
30	Creativity and You
31	Notes for Sharing This Book
32	Glossary

What Is Creativity?

Creativity is when you do things in a new way. You can be creative using your imagination and your body.

You are being creative when you paint a picture, write a story, or make up a dance.

Being creative doesn't mean that you must be the best at art or drama. Everyone can find ways to be creative, so have fun trying new things.

WHY IS CREATIVITY IMPORTANT?

In business, creativity is important. Creativity can help a business to attract customers, make better products, or stand out from the competition.

For you, a walk in nature could inspire creativity, or you might make up a fun and creative game to play with your friends.

What will our animal friends find out about creativity in business and about themselves?

Brainstorm Ideas

Milly Monkey's team is brainstorming ideas for an *epic* new zip line for Monkey Adventures. She wants them to be as creative as possible.

ALL ideas are welcome.

A dinosaur-themed zip line!

A loop-the-loop zip line!

A rocket-powered zip line!

Milly Monkey's team comes up with some fantastic ideas. Her only problem now is deciding which idea to choose.

Brainstorming creative ideas together is fun!

Have Fun Experimenting

Peter Panda decides to make new, exciting pizzas for his restaurant.

He has fun creating square pizzas, diamond pizzas, and star pizzas.

The ice-cream pizza Peter Panda tried to make didn't work. It melted in the oven and made a sticky mess!

But the other pizzas are a success. Peter's customers are excited to buy his fun and creative pizzas.

Have fun and be as creative as you can when experimenting.

Learn New Skills

Peggy Polar Bear creates beautiful ice sculptures. She thinks that making a huge ice bridge will be easy. But she soon realizes that she doesn't have the right skills.

After the training course, Peggy Polar Bear can't wait to try out the creative skills she's learned.

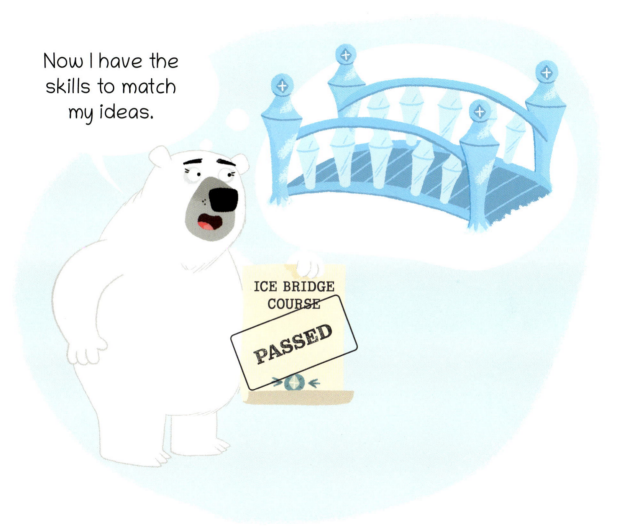

Now I have the skills to match my ideas.

Learning new skills helps your creativity.

Everyone Is Creative

Leon Lion wonders if selling cars can be as creative as his friends' businesses.

"Anyone can be creative if they try."

Leon looks at Pip Penguin's colorful hat and has a brilliant idea.

Everyone can be inspired to be creative.

Create Change

Kiki Koala planted a creative idea to get more customers to visit her tree farm.

Some customers come to buy trees. Other customers come to explore the maze. And many customers come to do both. Creativity helped Kiki Koala's business to change and grow.

Creativity can lead to exciting change.

Stand Out

Wei Wolf makes some very fancy hats. He thinks they're creative and fun, but not everyone agrees.

But Tilly Tiger can't wait to buy one.

Wei Wolf doesn't mind that not all customers love his hats. His business succeeds *because* it stands out.

Never be afraid to be yourself.

Be Inspired

Omar Owl's kite-making team has lost its creative spark. So, Omar takes them all for a team day out. A walk on a nature trail will help their creativity.

Back at the kite factory, the team makes creative kites inspired by what they saw today.

The world around you can inspire you to be creative.

Fail ... and Try Again

Chip Cheetah had some wild ideas about making his yoga classes more fun. But each new idea he tried went wrong.

But Chip Cheetah isn't afraid to fail. He keeps trying new ideas until he finds the perfect one for his business and customers.

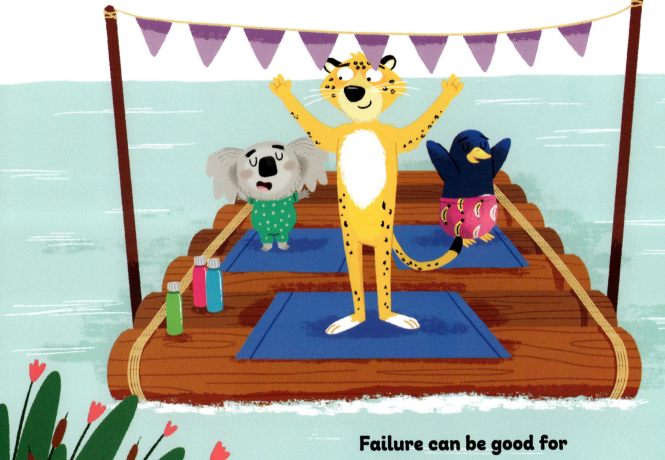

Failure can be good for creativity. Keep trying and you might surprise yourself.

Ask for Help

Pip Penguin is struggling to design a new logo for her ice-skating business. Luckily, she has an idea for how to get some creative help.

All the animals are excited to enter the competition.

Pip Penguin chooses Kit Kangaroo's logo as the winner.

If you feel stuck, ask for help.

Try New Ideas

Enzo Elephant is trying a creative new idea to help his toy shop business be more successful. Tonight is the first Toy Shop Play Night.

Customers can try as many toys as they like.
And they get a discount on any toys they want to buy.

The Toy Shop Play Night is a huge success!

Being creative sometimes means trying out new ideas.

Take a Break

Tilly Tiger is worried about her employee, Chip Cheetah. Chip is working too hard. He's very tired.

Chip relaxes in the fresh air, which makes him feel much better.

Now he doesn't feel so tired, Chip Cheetah feels creative again. He shows Tilly Tiger a new shoe design.

**It's hard to be creative when you feel tired.
Be kind to yourself and take a break.**

Celebrate Together

Kit Kangaroo entered her café's cake into the Animal Cake Championships.

Kit rushes up to collect the prize.

Suddenly, Kit Kangaroo remembers that Tilly Tiger spent the whole week baking and decorating the café's entry. Tilly's creativity helped them to win.

When you are creative with others, celebrate success together.

Creativity and You

Our animal friends have learned a lot about creativity in business. What they have learned can help you to be creative, too.

Omar Owl took his team out for the day.
Look at the world around you to inspire creative thinking.

Milly Monkey brainstormed with her team.
It's fun to be creative with others.

Chip Cheetah wasn't afraid to fail.
It's often more important not to give up than to get something right the first time. Creativity sometimes takes a bit of time and effort.

Notes for Sharing This Book

This book introduces business ideas around the topic of creativity. These ideas link to core personal and social growth skills, such as trying new things, feeling confident, and teamwork.

Talk to the child about what business is and why we need good businesses. You can use each scenario to discuss themes of creativity. For example, you could talk about the child's feelings around a time they felt frustrated while trying a creative activity.

Creativity works best when we feel positive. Learning new things also helps to develop creativity. Talk about a time when the child did something creative that they found challenging, such as writing a poem or creating art. What was the hardest part of being creative? How did they feel afterwards?

Glossary

brainstorm when a group of people discuss lots of ideas, often to solve a problem

business a company that buys, makes, or sells goods or services to make money

customer someone who buys things from a business

discount when a business sells a product or service at a lower price

employee someone who is paid wages (a set amount of money each week or month) to work for a business

experiment to try out new ideas, often not knowing how they will turn out

factory a place full of machines where a business makes lots of the same type of product

inspire to make someone feel like they want to do something

logo a symbol or design that a business uses to help customers identify the business

products the goods or services that a business makes or sells

training course a place where you learn extra skills or knowledge so that you can be better at doing something